RAYMOND A. HIRALDO

BE POET...
BE!

Trafford rev. 01/29/2015

www.trafford.com

North America & international
toll-free: 1 888 232 4444 (USA & Canada)
fax: 812 355 4082

Table of Contents

-Poems-

Table of Contents

-Poems-

-End Of Poems-

23 Chromosomes

There are 23 chromosomes in a female's egg and 23 in a male's sperm,
The sperm tries to get to the egg with a wiggle, and a worm,
Once the male's sperm finally meets up with the female's egg,
A baseball sized sphere soon grows from what used to be the size of a peg,

Nine months later, a baby is born, belonging to two parents,
A symbol of the combining of the two, which will harbor their many traits & talents,
Because that is what a baby is… one half, *one half* of the two!
It's something that happens after the coition of, "Me and You,"

But sometimes one parent won't see the chemical difficulty in creation,
And become convinced that life alone would reap a higher elation,
Forgetting that there are 23 similar chromosomes in the baby's total of 46,
Absent from the baby's life as a single parent's love becomes a temporary fix,

Because as soon as the child begins to speak at only a few years old,
It will ask a question that can make the tightest knitted heart unfold,
Then being a single parent after that will be like a golfer without a caddy,
As 23 chromosomes cry out for mommy, and 23 chromosomes cry out for daddy.

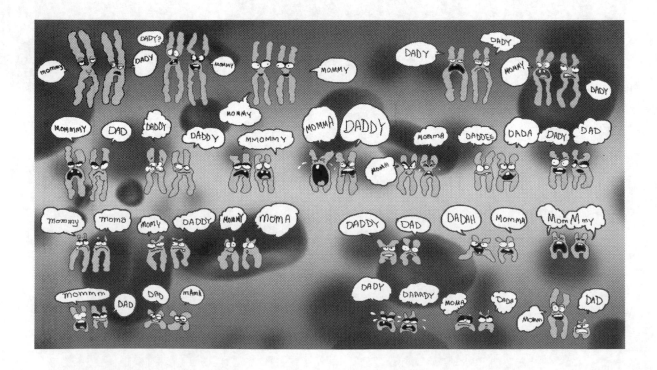

A Male's Curiosity

A cat and a man both share a similar kind of instinctual virtuosity,
And that *one* thing is an uncanny sense of tremendous curiosity,
But a male's curiosity is intensified to higher kinds of degrees,
It has helped him invent devices, and map the world's many seas,

However, it has also allowed him to fall into deep holes of trouble,
His curiosity is known to conceal the pits it makes with a giant shovel,
A female can spark the greatest curiosity inside of a male's head,
When he wonders about how any particular woman would look & feel like in bed,

A Male's Curiosity

He can be in the best relationship, but his curiosity will make his mind wander,
He can have the best car, but curiosity will make him ponder,
He'll wander away from his gorgeous brunette, and onto a beautiful blonde,
He'll dismiss his reliable vehicle, and go for something more, "James Bond,"

A cat will continue to strike at something with its furry little mitts,
Until that one thing hits it back, or scares it the heck out of its wits,
Curiosity can wipe out the coolest "cat," even before he can let off a final mew,
Because curiosity has been said to kill the cat, but many don't know that *it* buried him too.

A Poet's Desired Reaction

People might question the feasibility of a poet's numerous poetic letters,
Computers can try to analyze the words, but they will *all* get syntax errors,
The people that say, "This poem was nice," or "that poem was deep,"
Should might as well be fantasizing, or talking in their sleep,

They don't know the embedded emotions that poets put into their poems,
The feelings are like GIANTS, but cheap kudos turn them into gnomes,
Feeble compliments are things that poets do not want for their competence,
A sad or a happy tear instead, is a poet's desired reaction from the audience.

A Product

I heard it from one Dominican woman, and not from any form of "gentry,"
About how I am said to be a "product" of African ancestry,
Established in 1844 when it was named, "The Dominican Republic,"
My Dominican blood hides a truth that's only revealed when it runs thick,

Blood… it gushed from my ancestors by those involved in thieving loots,
Even though they were welcomed by sweet "Taino Indian" flutes,
I can just imagine all the horrible beatings, as my people were hit like drums,
Or when they spotted fields red, from their pricked enslaved thumbs,

My Dominican blood/culture is not pure; it is more of a combined mixture,
Which began a long time ago while being exposed to faith & proclaimed scripture,
It was unknown to me in mind, but, apparent in spirit,
I was so against it all that, I-I really didn't even want to hear it!

It was an approach from a Dominican woman before, but, I now have my own belief,
As the hidden truth in my blood is as real as the Santa Maria's demise on a reef,
It's something that I wasn't told by any White, Black, or Hispanic teacher or pastor;
That I am a product of a dark skin slave … raped by a White or Spanish master.

So I ask myself: "If some cultures are of each other and from each other … then, why would
they be against each other? Even till this day!"

A Species

Imagine a species that is both intelligent and ignorant,
Able to do things that are wicked, or magnificent,
A species that has the power to change the world almost overnight,
One that can hurt other organisms by causing destruction and blight,

Imagine a species that can bring others to extinction solely for their delectation,
A species that can destroy any surrounding… when they unite for a confrontation,
A species that waits for the very end to admit their wrongs with humility,
A species which knows that… with great power comes tremendous responsibility,

Despite all of this, they continue to kill off others for their own survival,
A mystical, lush, and fertile planet was greatly changed from their arrival,
Hint? This is a species that can understand all that is being spoken here,
It is a species that can control other species, and make them all feel fear,

They are hideous as well as beautiful, with promise and potential,
A species that can guide others… as they are extremely influential,
What kind of species could this be?! As if *it* couldn't be any clearer?
Want to know what this very authoritative species is? Easy, just look into a mirror…

A Whole From A Half

I am 180 degrees of unfinished love, as with you, I'd be a completed 360,
I've wanted 100 percent of life for so long, as without you, I only get 50,
We are like things that don't seem right when they are not together,
Like birds unable to fly ... if they don't have a single feather,

Like a grandfather clock's hypnotizing tick, but without a tock,
Or a golden key ... without a golden lock,
Like little children that don't pother,
Or no, "one hand that washes the other,"

No vehicle can go anywhere with only one half of a tire,
Much like the distance you won't get if you tried swimming in a mire,
Without you, there's a part of me still in its infancy, needing its bib,
As I am a man who is desperately searching for his long lost rib,

For only *you*—my woman—can complete me and make me whole,
And return to me a piece of love that a thief called "loneliness" stole,
During coitus we create a power that rivals the one from the archangel "St. Michael,"
Because as I enter your wet orifice, & you kiss into my oral desire, we generate love's cycle.

Agony With Someone New

You've left someone who is now an "ex," and are in the process of seeing a new person,
But there is a slight feeling of discomfort, as you're exposed to this conversion,
Of total strangers becoming acute of one another as they get mentally involved,
This time invested in each other passes as quickly as sand in a liquid... being dissolved,

This is the "getting to know you" phase, and without a doubt, it is time consuming,
As you're a bit scared to be your *total* self while you both admire flowers blooming,
Then, suddenly there are thoughts racing through your mind's "mental chasm,"
About how if you were with your "ex," this day would end with a certain "gasm,"

Then, you begin:
Wondering if this new person will accept the habits that your "ex" had tolerated,
Hoping that the same love you'll give this new person will be totally reciprocated,
Yearning to want to be nuttier than a fruitcake, without later being tossed,
Wanting to laugh after dinner and *not* care of the fact that you haven't flossed,
Craving explanations that you already know won't end up being deceptive,
Dying to feel your "ex" in bed, without too much thought of a contraceptive,

Because your body physically recognizes your "ex," and has little left to be known,
It feels comfortable no matter if your "ex" has had his/her ice cream on a different cone,
You try to listen to the new person, but find you have become visually & audibly impaired,
As you find yourself thinking about your "ex" and analyzing how he/she compared,

Meeting the new person's family actually gives you a feeling of concern than that of a treat,
Because you don't know if you can gain the confidence of the new strangers you will meet,

The term "starting over" always comes with a distinctive kind of weight,
But it is a lot more profound when used in conjunction with the loss of a mate,
All this is rather obvious but many individuals don't admit it through and through,
That it's agony trying to reach the level you were at with your "ex," with someone new.

I feel that this is a subconscious reason why so many people make up, after a break up.

Ahora

Me parece que la mujer hermosa de hoy no quiere un hombre bueno ... como yo,
Prefería estar con un hombre que siempre daña to…
Ella no quiere un hombre que siempre está preocupado por cómo ella está haciendo,
Es como si ella odia un hombre sincero, y se fascina con el hombre que le está mintiendo,

Y hay una cosa que siempre sucede, y a veces me hace reír,
Cuando ella se junta con un hombre malo, que solo la hace sufrir,
Entonces *ahora*, en este tiempo, cuando nada se puede hacer,
Ella se siente aprisionada con ese hombre, porque tienen un bebé,

Cómo han pasado los años, y ella se da cuenta de que ella no tiene nada,
Y por eso ella siempre tiene pesadillas, y se despierta descontrolada,
Cómo ese hombre le ha dado un corazón más frío que un cubo de hielo,
Ella rogándole a Dios que la mate para que, al menos, podía sentir el amor en el cielo

Pero el momento en que ella se da cuenta de que Dios no mata en sangre fría,
Ella me verá con una mujer agradecida, que demuestra *gran* alegría,
Entonces será *ahora* que ella quiere un hombre bueno ... como yo,
Porque ahora, con lágrimas en los ojos, ella sabe que yo le habría dado to…

To … *todo* lo mejor—de amor, de mí, y de la vida.

<u>All I Have To Do</u>

Deep inside I've always felt that you liked tranquility, and not commotion,
And how you despise cheaters, which is why *I* offer you devotion,
I know we haven't had the best relationship, so, I'm asking for a clean slate,
Because, I love you, and all I have to do is *hear* your voice, & I am great.

Baby, I have never been materialistic so, don't go crazy with souvenirs,
I don't need sunglasses from "Chanel," nor do I want jewelry from "De Beers,"
I just love to be with you on your elegant days or days you call, "Yucky,"
For all I have to do is just *look* at you, and I begin to feel *so* lucky.

This is the hardest time to try to find a special someone with morals,
As everyone wants to be right, and thus, engage in stupid quarrels,
This is why I respect you and your intelligence to the *fullest* degree!
And all I have to do is just *talk* with you to feel so accepted and free.

You may think I am crazy when I don't want to have sex,
As I am sure you think that *it* is a man's sole reflex,
Or times when I don't hug & kiss you in places that are "public" or "discreet,"
But it's just that, all I have to do is be next to you, and I *already* feel complete.

Apparently

This is for those individuals who don't know that they are the newly "up and comers,"
The ones born to be great, regardless if they become movie stars or plumbers,
Understand that a person unknown to many can still be successfully rich,
Because every single person has their very own destined niche,

So if an aspiring actress wonders, "Who'd want to see me in roles of various types?"
Or if a new craftsman thinks, "Who'd pay me well for fixing some dumb ol' broken pipes?"
Apparently, millions will flock to theaters to see her in her first big acting role,
Apparently, thousands will dial his number when a pipe is leaking water over a bowl.

Apparently ...

Like the privates in boot camp who never thought they'd become elite contras,
There is always room for plenty more, in many fields, *and* in different genres,
Move forward, especially if you believe that you'll succeed where others have failed,
Because apparently there are individuals out there whose fate will never be curtailed.

Apparently ...

So, if you think that no-one would be interested in reading your stories of catastrophe,
Understand that people *will* notice your writing, right down to each apostrophe.
In the world, you will find that no genre could ever become totally saturated,
People claim to have seen & heard it all, but continue to be amazed at the underrated.

Apparently! Right? ☺

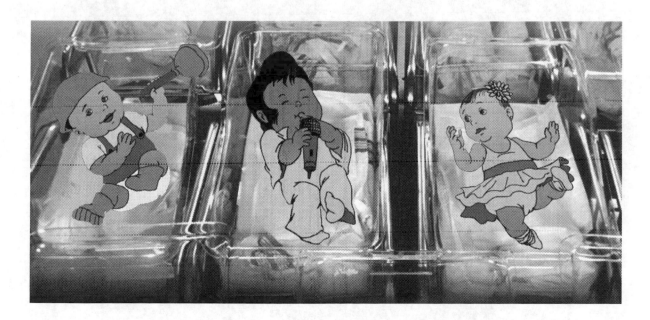

<u>At 3 AM</u>

It's *such* a drag at how it often hits me at 3 AM in the morning,
At a time when my family and friends are in their beds... snoring!
The people that tell me to call them whenever I'm feeling depressed,
Told me to call them no matter the time, and promised that they won't protest,

How it hits me the hardest when no-one is around,
And how *it* always comes up, when I'm feeling safe and sound,
Depressed at something that happened to me last month, or maybe even last year,
And so begins that deep thinking walk that I wish could finish at the home of a peer.

I'm here questioning why this usually happens to me at 3 AM in the morning,
When it just comes rushing out, without even giving me a warning.
My heart feels *so* heavy, as if something is weighing it down,
Similar to being pulled underwater, and soon starting to drown.

No-one is with me at this moment, when it is my greatest time of need,
When sweet words can become sunlight to depression's vampires as they come to feed,
The telephone looks like a boulder when I think about the question,
Of what the person on the other line will think of me, because of *this* depression.

The way that they will listen to me as if they are in a sound altering pod,
Reacting to my every word with a "Mmmhmm," wishing I could hear their head nod,
Never really thinking for a brief moment that the words they might be ignoring,
Are my pleas asking them to help me, so that this isn't my final 3 AM in the morning.

Athlete

I was practically born cutting the ribbon that a first place runner breaks at the end of a race,
My heart already knew how to calm itself from a hard exercising pace,
Even before my conception, I *knew* the way victory would taste,
Competition was like a chicken, that I already knew how to baste,

I am an athlete, born to compete!
Designed to be classified under "elite!"
Perfect my very *own* effective technique,
While building a strong & muscular physique.

Some people get jealous and believe that I'm a drug user,
If I degrade myself to that then, I'm *already* a loser,
NO! I am a natural athlete who will never *ever* cheat!
I will keep my diet wholesome, nutritious and complete!

I'll train harder every single day and go an extra length,
To max out my power, my will, and my strength.
I'll help out the weak when they fall into a physical trench,
And provide them with the winning tools to kill that "failing stench."

I am the athlete who people will always see on top,
My winning streak won't slow down, *nor* will it come to a stop,
I am the one everyone will see in the media while they shop,
Getting up from a fall, *if* ever I drop.

For I am an athlete who was born to compete,
Not afraid to spill my blood on hard textured concrete,
Engulf everyone with my winning mystique,
Don't give a damn about *any* kind of critique.

There is *nothing* quite like the feeling of wearing a gold medal in front of a heart that gave its all.

Bare Bones

If a man said that he'd never want a woman's sex then, he is a liar and a cad!
Because every human being wants to have sex so much that, it often feels *so* bad,
Even the most humbled nun, or the most devoted priest,
Prays hourly for God to forgive their inner sexual beast.

People who have experienced it will say that it's a rule of their thumbs,
That a human body feels so much better during, *and* after it "cums,"
It is the motions during sex and the start of any penetration,
That brainwashes any mind away from thoughts of degradation,

Then nothing becomes too "freaky," "dirty," or "disgusting,"
As both genders don't care if it is "love making" or "lusting,"
If a man & a woman are left alone together for enough time, something *will* happen,
Sooner or later, sex will be evident from the sound of a pelvis and buttocks thwappin'.

Males unlock females, as women are the golden doors to procreation,
And just their presence alone pushes a male towards sexual activation,
So along with hormonal changes & a subconscious attraction of pheromones,
A man & a woman always desire to be together, right down to their bare bones.

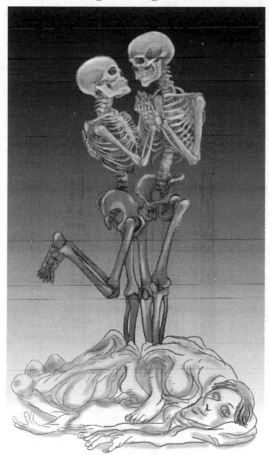

Be Poet Be

Write poet, write!

Write about all the things that certain people keep inside,
Write about all their feelings, from being happy to terrified,
Write the one thousand words that a picture is said to be worth,
Write about a world's abundance of love & its nourishing limits of dearth!

Feel poet, feel!

Feel the magmatic emotions of many individualistic volcanoes,
Feel how some earn "Yeses" in their lives while others obtain "noes,"
Feel the ones around you, from those here now and those gone too soon,
Feel the miracle of channeling their vibes from you being so well in tune.

Look poet, look!

Look to the night sky and witness the stars of an enormous spiral galaxy,
Look into the pupils of those who speak the truth and also fallacy,
Look closely at both to realize very similar kinds of twinkles,
Look at life's amazements in sparkling dots above epidermic wrinkles.

Listen poet, listen!

Listen to the many that'll laugh and mock you with criticism or ridicule,
Listen to things crucial & giant, or things unimportant & miniscule,
Listen to the voices around you and those deep within,
Listen to all that you hear, pay attention, now begin…

Begin writing about everything that seems simple or challenging
Begin feeling the mysterious energy your words will be unraveling
Begin looking for the small poetic clues in every kind of activity
Begin listening to inspiration as it brings you agitation or tranquility.

Bare your mind, bare your heart, bare your soul, bare *yourself* if it gets your message across.
But be poet... BE!

Before & After

I sparked her interest after I made a cute comment of her red dress,
My desire's scale told me that she'd be a ten, and *nothing* less,
I had a love history before I met her—it was torn, cold, and bitter,
Having her beauty beside me often made me feel like a home run hitter.

I've never felt such a level of comfort when our relationship blossomed & grew,
I was my *total* self around her, something prior women couldn't make me do,
We had more ups and downs than a river being tried by a white water rafter,
And they made me think that my life was okay before her, and it'd be okay after.

But upon us breaking up & me being without her... I fell into a strong state of withdrawal,
She now being official with someone else brought me a great feeling of appall,
Only because I know that her new man is going to benefit from her goodness;
He's going to love her attention & care, as she was like a private stewardess.

I know I began pushing her away when I stopped being overzealous,
And now I have to admit that I have become overly jealous,
Why? Because her new man is going to benefit from all the help I gave her,
And he is going to experience a pleasure from her that is warmer than wool or fur.

No ex-man wants to know of another man getting close to what he once held so passionately,
It is something that I can totally admit—with my male heart—*adamantly,*
I felt unique when I made her laugh so hard that her wheeze sounded like a sparrow's tweet,
I later found out that this other man made the same thing happen by the third week,

I know she probably thought no-one else could bring out her unique kind of laughter,
Now I have to accept the fact that she had a life before "us," and she'll surely have one after.

It hurts at just the thought of once memorable items being replaced, or even filling a garbage can. But nonetheless, I wish her nothing but luck & happiness with the person she allows to occupy her future.

Believe In Love

I find it odd at how some people see love as annoying as "ribbits" or croaks,
I often wonder if some people *truly* mean what they say in marital jokes,
Despite cupid torturing me every February when he leaves me without a valentine,
I still believe in love as powerfully as the religion practiced in Palestine.

Inside of my veins flows a sweet red river that powers my heart's drill,
But it lacks the strength to penetrate a female heart that has a doubtful will,
Because two hearts need to believe in love for both of them to safely fall,
For if one is in love and the other isn't then, that relationship will surely stall.

I still believe in love because, I just *can't* be the only one who feels this way!
And if I change too drastically then, I'll destroy the chance of having it one day,
Because if I do meet up with it as someone I'm not then, it won't think that I need love,
For it'll ask me a question that I could only get right if I be-lieve-in love.

And so I continue to wait for the day when I can show and tell it on an altar that, I do!

Carpe Diem

Its definition marks an action we should all do when we wake up, & that's, "seize the day,"
Because you literally need to "gather ye rosebuds while ye may,"
So when you look to the morning sky & see a faded moon in its quarterly crescent,
That's a celestial wink implying, "you're welcome," towards a new day present,

When you start your day & see a great opportunity you *need* to exercise carpe diem,
No matter if it's in an early AM time or within the late hours of PM,
Be aware that unique opportunities will only manifest themselves once,
And you don't want to lose that chance & gain the title of "dunce,"

If you spot a person that attracts you, then, you need to exercise carpe diem,
Because nothing will guarantee you another time that you will get the chance to see 'em,
Whether you are rejected or accepted is another thing, but, look at it this way,
I bet you when you turn in at night you'll be glad that you seized the day.

Each day is like a gift wrapped present, open it!

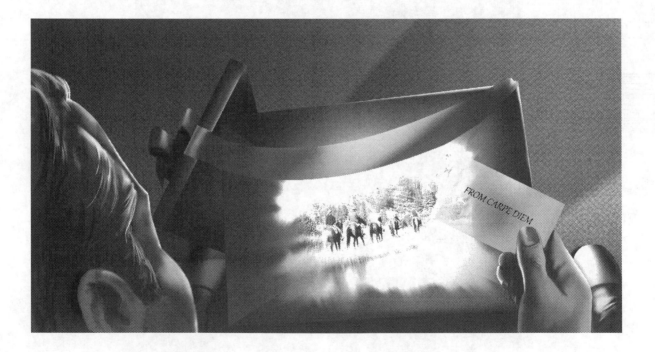

Coming Clean

What I'm about to say may hurt you, but, I need to come clean,
Please understand that I am not doing this to be mean,
I honestly feel that our relationship never had love in it from the beginning,
It was a mistake to think love would surface if we allowed it to keep spinning,

Don't blame yourself because you gave me the best kind of affection,
And no, this isn't about the insecurities you have of your figure or your skin's complexion,
It's just that, being unsure about someone you're with brings opaque goals & low self-esteem,
And long single lives made us dive into lust's paint as we thought it was love's ice cream,

Our main faults were that I didn't give you enough time, & you were too possessive,
Sacrificing school & work days to see each other was okay at first, but later got too aggressive,
Now, please don't say that I was only with you to fulfill the human urges of sex,
Because *both* of our thirsts for flesh could be compared to that of a Tyrannosaurus Rex,

I know we covered the unprotected sex topic like soapy water over grime,
But raw intimacy can overshadow the consequences of becoming parents before our time,
Your "I love you" threw my mind into a spin that hasn't stopped reeling,
Because those powerful words propelled "us" to a level that I just wasn't feeling,

Each time you told me those words, you would wait to see if I'd say them back,
So I said them emptily, because I felt anything else would've been like a stinging smack,
It was wrong to look into your eyes and say a phony "I love you,"
When what I should've said was that I love the things you do,

I know you wanted to hear this face to face instead of over the phone,
I just couldn't understand why, even though I was with you, I *still* felt alone,
You must think of how heartless I am, but, these are things I could no longer conceal,
I know everything I said sounded harsh but, I just can't sugarcoat the way I feel,

I don't blame you for casting me into your heart's dungeon after I sat on its throne,
But it's not right to be with someone just for the sake of not wanting to be alone.

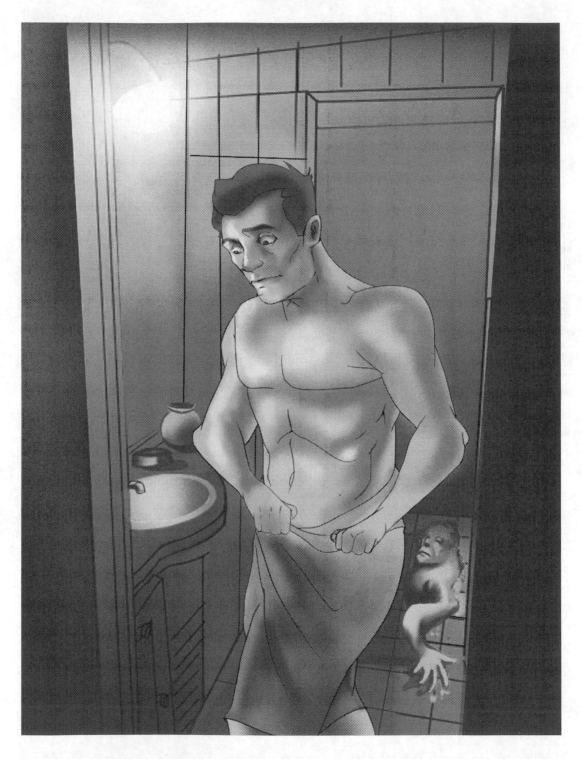

Feeling better the next day, after washing away the phony me with a bar of words.

Cultural Red Flag

I think that an inter-cultural relationship is a beautiful thing,
To see two totally different individuals together, & enjoying each other's zing,
However, I can't help but to challenge what brought about this cultural stray,
As I often see particular cultured women look at "their own" men with appall or dismay,

No professional Black, or Hispanic woman wants a man that's more angled than a bevel,
Which is why she'll look outside of her culture for someone straight, *and* at her level,
This being the case, there is now a need for a cultural red flag,
To stop the antics of Black & Hispanic men, & the time they use to brag,

Hispanic men, all of you *seriously* need to up-up your antes,
And show our latinas that we can do more than just try to dive into their panties,
More of us need to become decorated lawyers and top notch doctors,
We need to be the engineers who design bridges, & the pilots who fly helicopters,

We need to stop giving our mami chulas a reason to throw a cultural red flag!

Black men, y'all *really* need to relax with all those insanely violent rhyming chants,
And show your women that you can pick up your slack, *and* also your pants!
You need to show your ebony beauties that life won't be constant struggles or strains,
You always flaunt your bodies to them, now show them the muscle of your brains,

You need to stop giving your honeys a reason to throw a cultural red flag!

Now, there is nothing wrong with "arroz & cabbage" being served back to back,
And coffee tastes great with cream, and also when it is black,
Nothing wrong with having plantains along with grits,
Love can take the oddest shape, & show the world how well it fits,

But that face that a Black or Latino man puts when they see how "their" women have bailed,
Is not a look of jealousy, or racism, but a look that brings a feeling of how they've failed!

Failed to be what "their own" women want, failed to be what "their own" women need, and
failed to prevent a cultural red flag.

Cultures

The same way every human mouth has an individual bite,
Each culture—within the human race—is special in its own right.

From the voice and strength of Blacks,
To great Arab writings on stones or plaques,
There are cultures that have been truly historic.

From the leadership & unity of Caucasian,
To the intelligent and talented Asian,
There are cultures that continue to be incredibly influential.

From Hispanic love & pride,
To Indian sensuality that's well applied,
There are cultures instilled with the hottest fires of passion.

And much like unexplored regions only visited by winds harshly blown,
There are cultures that till this day are still very much unknown,
All cultures first began with mystery.

Dear Terrorist

Dear Terrorist:

We, the American people, don't understand your actions,
They are *beyond* anything we call, "felonies," or "infractions,"
All we know is that they fall under merciless anger,
And our world doesn't need a vile & ruthless mangler,

We are sickened at how you think a person's life is like a marble,
And were you particularly jealous of our tall twin marvel?
The pain you have made us feel leaves us with no kind of descriptive word,
But here are a few voices that *need* to be heard...

Terrorist, I am the sister of that man you executed,
He was a great teacher, with a record that was undisputed,
How could you put out a brilliance that only wanted to enlighten your civilization?
He wanted to help your people realize their dreams, & help to enrich your nation.

Terrorist, we are the parents of that young man whom you used as a ploy,
He was so anxious to heed your country's calls for help, as he was *such* a good boy,
You have destroyed our generation with your actions of a lion in the wild,
We are both too old to have any more children, and *he* was our only child.

Dear American people, Sister and Parents:

I was just as civil as all of you are,
I lived peacefully, with no intentions to mar,
But how would you feel if a stranger came into your home & began giving you orders?
And *that* is the first thing you American people did when you crossed into my borders.

I have enough right to my own way of living as every single one of you,
As your government wants to paint my skies green, when they *need* to stay blue,
I have a different way of life that just *cannot* function under your bureaucracy,
And I have strict religious laws that are rejected by your "democracy,"

I have lost not one family, but *several* in your government's greed,
And I don't want to be a follower of the mightiest country that has the lead,
Our children here are thought of differently than from over there,
Over here they are not just children, but someone else's heir.

I have often felt like a sheep that is being robbed of its fleece,
As you Americans think that you *are* the world's police!
So you can call me a "terrorist," as I see every *single* one of you as a heathen!
You all currently feel but a small bit of my pain, so for now, *we* are even.

Terrorists are not born, they are made.

Deceased Sinner

The only thing moving on him is hair, as it was caught in a windy gust,
His lifeless body is now on display, before it goes back to its former dust,
Will he be ready to meet the Lord? And will he be accepted by the creator?
Or will the heavenly father cast him away, while shouting the word, "traitor"?

The sinner finds himself before a supreme glow, as it shines above a mighty altar,
He is questioned lovingly, but an extreme guilt makes his speech falter,
He braves the brilliant pure golden light, and manages to see what looks like a shoulder,
He tilts his head left, then right, but his movements were stopped before they grew bolder,

Could it be possible to peek over God to see what awaits the chosen few?
He covers his flash blinded eyes & looks away, as impurity cannot withstand the golden hue,
And *there!* He now sees his loved ones who have passed away, and he yearns to be kissed,
The eyes of God fill with burning tears as angelic hands lead him away by each wrist.

Where is he going? Or worse yet, where has he gone?
Will love be present there? Along with beautiful sunrises at dawn?
How will he know if it is real? And what if his time isn't *really* over?
Will he wake up drunk among strangers again? Or in pain, fully sober?

Material worldly things, or God's promise of eternal life, which one did he choose?
Bright red lights begin trailing him, slithering like sparks on a dangling fuse,
The angels take him through a passageway that has a putrid smell of sulfur,
He begins to feel a burn from within his stomach that is worse than the rawest ulcer,

He starts to hear the loudest kinds of torture induced screams,
He tugs at the angelic robes so hard that he temporarily straightens out their perfect seams,
He began to choke as he was taken alongside the edge of a fear gripping cliff,
This new smell made what he had smelled before seem just like a tiny whiff,

The angels dematerialized and thus, disappeared from his sides,
Along with the reassuring protection that emanated from his divine guides,
He heard, "do you want to live again?" in which he replied with a shout of, "YES! PLEASE!"
He was shown a portal to re-enter his body at its wake, but it was just a demonic tease,

What did the filthy sinful life he had lived on earth allow him to acquire?
A new world—without God—surrounded by serpents, demons, and a lake of fire!

Deceased Sinner

Decisions

There comes a time in which you need to decide on a path,
Sometimes that decision is delayed, when you think about its aftermath,
Decisions are inevitable in life, and grow harder with the years,
And supreme uneasiness comes as a decision making moment nears,

Take me for example, I recently bought a brand new car that is technologically mainstream,
This is a car I would talk about constantly, and it was basically in my every dream,
I was getting rid of the current one I had because of its annoying engine ping,
To my greatest surprise the brand new car also has the same annoying thing!

I broke up with a great woman because I had strong feelings for another,
The other woman then began revealing bad habits, and that made me think less of her,
But it wasn't until I had issues with the other woman that I began thinking about my true loss,
As the other woman loves to force things on me, as if she was my life's boss,

In a world where decisions can make or break your coming future events,
They need to occur, no matter if they cause ventricular scars or mental dents,
But the worst thing about *any* decision that has the potential to reward or stun,
Is the time you waste in thinking about it when you are trying to make one.

Decisions… Decisions… Decisions!

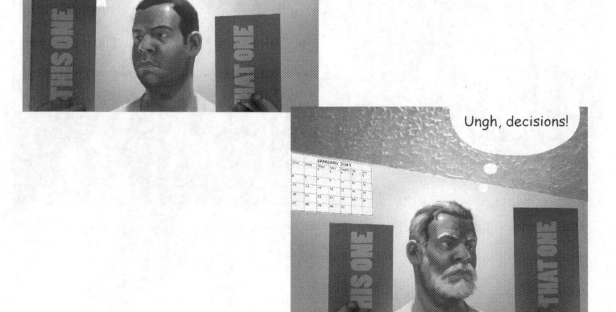

Disregarding Life

After numerous rejections & failures, I felt that life sucked for sure!
And that death was the only thing which was its permanent cure,
I thought about inhaling the exhaust from my car, as I parked it & let it idle,
But I wanted to die "naturally," as I couldn't bring myself to being suicidal,

So I began disregarding my life's actions, without thinking of any consequences,
Not caring if I punctured my scrotum for climbing over barbed wire fences,
From sneaking into places that denied access to every other civilian,
As I knew that my chances of survival in these areas were about one out of a million,

But I didn't stop there! I began having unprotected sex with all the women I dated,
I shouted, "F--K OFF!" to people who loathed me, and to all the ones I hated,
I bungee jumped off of bridges, without caring about breaking the bungee cord,
I skydived out of planes, from altitudes where no types of birds have soared,

I drove high horsepower cars & rode motorcycles at ridiculous velocities,
I laughed at the faces of fear, danger, and all kinds of different atrocities,
I felt like my life was extended on purpose, as my age went from 29 to 110,
Then *it* manifested itself to me, and I said, "Finally!" as before I questioned, "When?"

Get this! Death actually came to me apologizing, as it said that it was finally my time,
I told it: "I hope my ride in your ferry boat is free because I'm not giving you a dime!"
I went for another shot that I hoped would make death's bones boil,
"Hey death, I can hear your bones crackling like rice cereal, maybe you need some oil!"

Death just stared at me while holding on to its long sharp sickle,
I could tell that my jokes were far from making it feel any kind of tickle,
Then something occurred to me as death looked unamused, standing next to my bedpost,
That upon me disregarding life—not caring if I died—was when in fact, I lived the most!

And now that I was happy with prior thoughts of adventure & courage from within my life is
when death came, and deep inside, it *actually* found me wanting to continue to live.

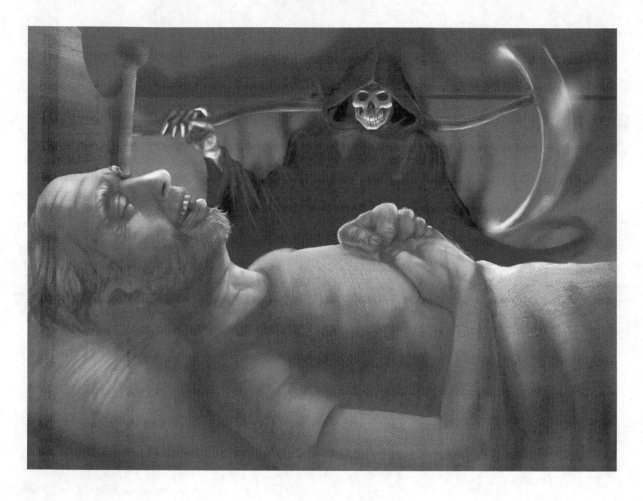

I might be crazy but, I think death *actually* respects those souls that do not fear it.

Famous Yet

I can do what I want because, well, I am not famous yet,
That means I can go into strip clubs, or go to a race track and place a bet,
People haven't seen me on TV or anything so, I can do *whatever* I please,
I could go into any park at night and urinate on the trees,

I can scream at the top of my lungs with the most horrible curse,
And I can drive around the city naked with my car's shifter in reverse,
I would be able to shrug off a fall on a floor that was slippery when wet,
People will laugh but they won't remember me, because I am not famous yet,

I don't have to worry about my face being in the late evening news,
With the headline reading, "Mr. So and So fell down and lost his shoes,"
I can go into any bar and drink a beer,
Without a crowd shouting, "Hey! Mr. So and So is here!"

I can shout out anything I want because, I am not famous yet,
I—"Excuse me sir but, we're waiting for you, service has cleaned & refueled your jet."
How dare that little peasant pilot interrupt me, he is such an ignoramus!
Oops! I better watch what I say, for a minute there I forgot that I was famous.

Fancy Meeting You Here

You're heading off to work—after you overslept—& you're mad about running late,
Your feeling of being upset doesn't allow you to see this intended part of fate,
An attractive person loses their glasses and you notice their vision is totally unclear,
You hand fate's glasses back to them as your heart shouts, "fancy meeting you here!"

Life can be compared to a game called, "Tetris" in which every move is critical,
Gaps left at the bottom of the game's stack can make everything appear pitiful,
But with patience you'll find ways to make the best of the game's grooves,
And realize the errors you made earlier will contribute positively to your next moves,

Errors in life exist so that you can be sculpted into the person you need to become,
They bring about a humbled sense of knowledge, regardless if you find them dumb,
You'll spend more time not believing you made the error as another one draws near,
But soon you realize it's destiny as your mind speaks, "fancy meeting you here,"

There is *always* a reason to understand why things happen the way they do,
If only we'd stop to analyze some things before seeing them in a negative view,
Most times we act on impulse like the soreness of a tongue after it was bitten,
And this is the worst time to admit that your whole life is basically already written,

A source of monetary income is as necessary as the air that we inhale,
Losing that particular source is just flat out beyond the pale,
Upon losing the job you attempt to drown your sourness with a newspaper & a beer,
Opportunity shows up as a job ad as your qualifications say, "fancy meeting you here,"

Life is full of chance, luck, opportunity, destiny and fate,
Life tends to throw these things towards us at the proper time or date,
So even those people viewed as ignorant, or even the ones who are deemed as "wise,"
Are all caught off guard by "fancy meeting you here," also known as ...

Fancy Meeting You Here

(yep, I'm pretty sure you guessed it) a blessing in disguise! ☺

<u>Fireworks</u>

I'm at a place where people don't seem to care if these mosquitoes are carrying malaria,
Because that won't stop hundreds of people from being in this open area,
I'm here in a trance, trying to absorb the smallest detail of my observation,
As everyone is celebrating the independence of a great & inspiring nation,

I'm sitting on a park bench, and I inhale the crispness of the air as I close my eyes,
When I open them after exhaling lightly, I'm treated to the dance of fireflies,
It is now 8:45 PM on this July 4th, 2005, as I can feel the air getting cooler,
I notice a happy little girl in front of me, riding around on a silver toy scooter,

I'm just here, trying to be poetic before the start of Macy's July 4th fireworks display,
An event that makes so many people rush to viewing areas without any type of delay,
And here they start as I see the first one going up in the distance!
As this park is now a special place, where people treasure their admittance,

But while I'm here witnessing this huge extravaganza,
My mind deters away, as I am shown my next stanza,
The fireworks now help me envision how love should be,
As they continue to explode ... so thunderously!

How the one that started it all had its own unique burst,
As in love when ... no other could *ever* compare to the first,
How love makes me persistent to find it, like the trails of firework shells launched before,
How it will always leave me so thirsty for its excitement, and desperate to get some more,

I just want to romance one woman, & *so* much that, cupid will call her a spoiled brat,
But funny how cupid always plays games when it knows where your heart is at,
Because cupid knows that it will always catch me with every single little joke,
As fireworks show me love's beauty, power, & lasting influence with light, sound, & smoke.

Fireworks

For Us Good Men

This poem is dedicated to us romantically good men who stay devoted,
The ones whose hearts are *so* sweet they could very well be sugarcoated,
This is for us good men who go above & beyond love's call of duty,
The ones who still hug & kid with their woman, no matter if she's moody,

This is for us good men who may appear weak or easily shaken,
Whose true manly intentions come forth when they are lovingly taken,
This is for us good men who'd do anything to satisfy their woman's needs,
Who bathe her in a flood of pure & loving water—that neither runs dry nor recedes,

This is for us good men who still write love poems & romantic notes,
The ones that even years later, are *still* as playful as billy goats,
This is for us good men who aren't afraid to let love overcome their neutrons,
Who would drive for miles to get their woman's favorite salad, with special croutons,

And this is for us good men who still have no-one to do these things to,
Who are looked upon (by some women) as if each one of us were a silly cockatoo.
This is for us good men who see February 14th more than once a year,
Who float to their woman's side when she softly says, "Come here,"

And I tell you… fellas, whether we are lost in love, or stranded in loneliness, *we* are worth more than bars of gold.

So, this is for *us*, good men!

From Africa With Love

The human race will never admit the possibility of it originating from one location,
Being from how different we all look in each continent & in every nation,
There is just nothing that can be said to bring about any type of persuasion,
No word that can convince others of this possible implication,

Except… "Love."

A group of scientists screened hundreds of people at a local street fair,
Taking painless swab samples to trace their DNA origins from, ev-er-y-where!
The samples were transported for research & kept safe in depositories,
Upon arriving they were analyzed in different laboratories,

The result? Each person's ancestry was traced back to a location in Africa.

So to the light skinned people who can't believe they came from those whose skin is dark,
Take a moment, look at your bodies and find a black spot known as a, "birth mark,"

That's from Africa, with love.

To the people with beautifully dead straight hair, which stems from your scalps,
Ever wondered why certain strands of it stick up? Almost as high as the Swiss Alps?!
Those strands are alive with DNA as they often make your stylist unhappy,
But that lively kind of hair shares coding from hair that's considered to be nappy,

From Africa, with love.

In Africa you will find so many types of friendly tribes,
That have no urge for money, & no use for tricky bribes,
They'll hug & welcome you, because deep down they'll feel what I've previously stated,
As those tribes people feel that there's a good chance you & them could be related,

So, welcome back to your originating home, from Africa, with love!

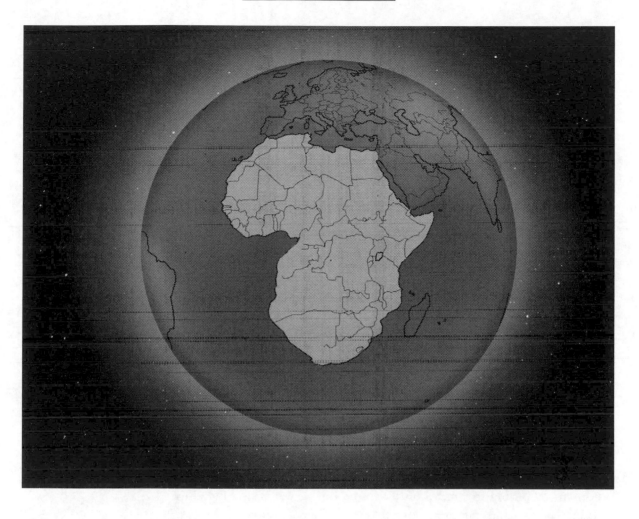

Good Foot Forward

I know men see her as someone who appears to be beautiful & generous,
They could never think of her as being vindictive or venomous,
But her superficial beauty could brainwash even the most cunning,
Leaving them unwilling to think about any peril that could be coming,

If other men knew what this man knows, they'd stop *dead* in their tracks,
And they would put a zipper lock on every pocket in their slacks,
On top of that, they would learn to always carry a bottle of visine,
To protect their eyes from the sting of her hidden bad hygiene,

I wish I would have been given some form of warning sign,
Before getting with her after thinking how she was so fine,
Because now I see that she's insecure, ill-mannered and extremely froward,
And how upon meeting a new man, she'll always put her good foot forward,

If other men knew what I know, they would literally turn and run away from her!

Women flock to him because he dresses nice & sounds educated in speech,
He gives off this impression of having his goals & dreams within his reach,
His taste in fashion & style could turn even the most unwilling female head,
As that woman is like a mouse caught in a snake's trance without one word being said,

If those women knew what this woman knows, they'd turn their cheeks as he'd pass,
And not even listen to a single word of all the great qualities he will say he has,
I didn't mind paying for things until I found out he was just being cheap,
And I'd even see him taking money from me when I pretended to be asleep,

I wish I would have been given some form of warning sign,
Before he got me drunk with his words of pure moonshine,
Because now I see that he's a deadbeat loser, with actions that are just awkward,
But how upon meeting a new woman, he'll always put his good foot forward,

If other women knew what I know, they would ready the pepper spray & keep on walking!

Note to selves Always give yourselves enough time to *really* get to know someone!

Grading Energy

I just felt energy as strong as a leader's words of deep proclamation,
My heart translated it to: "A grading energy based on a person's occupation,"
I felt it from a woman's mind, as it assumed that I was lost in all kinds of miseries,
"He is cute," I felt from her, along with, "But it's too bad he does deliveries!"

As fine as she was, I'd say too bad for her if she longs for someone to hold her respectfully.

For love tells me that, in it all, happiness is all that would really matter,
As my current occupation makes me spread around like fallen beads that scatter,
Yes, I was making a delivery to someone else inside that store,
But what if love was delivering me to her so that we could be together forever more?

Grading Energy

I guess I needed to feel this energy, as it did not want to escape detection,
An energy I felt was the essence of Darwin's theory of natural selection,
It was an energy that I can describe as feeling so undeniably degrading!
It discouraged me from telling her any words that could've been persuading,

And I've actually felt this "grading energy" in other different places as well,
Being given off from me towards women who work in McDonalds or Taco Bell,
This grading energy is responsible for so many of my heart's unnecessary murders,
As it spoke, "She is pretty, but too bad she mops floors or flips burgers,"

Too bad for the aching love in my heart when I radiated that grading energy,
As it was only a matter of time before it was radiated directly back towards me.

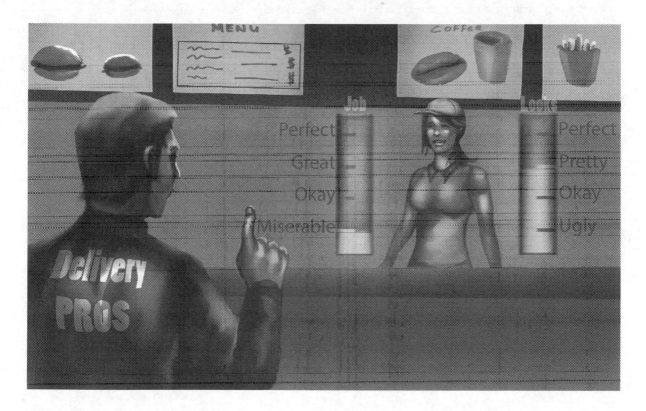

This energy made me wonder. If all of us were to be unemployed, with no types of professions, & no job titles, then, we would *all* just be employees of life.

Holy Proof

I don't know why certain people claim to be atheist or agnostic,
As holy proof can be found in letters of words viewed normally, or acrostic,
We can say certain things, and never realize that their origins are holy,
And most times these are terms that are actually used solely,

We have "Christmas" for example—just look at the name—how could *it* be better evident?
The giving of meaningful things on that day makes it all the more relevant,
Jesus Christ is meaningful to man, even though man prefers the things he can savor,
Eerie coincidence then that most Christmas gifts are not always viewed as "in favor?"

So! Christmas *is* holy proof!

Uncover the earlier dates that are referred to as, "primeval,"
So you can unknowingly realize a holy retrieval,
Can you now believe in his existence? As your eyes will undoubtedly see,
How Christ is acknowledged in any past date that ends with, "B.C."

Ready for more holy proof?

If people analyzed the saying of, "March comes in like a lion & goes out like a lamb,"
Some will wonder why it couldn't go out more like a dove, or even a clam,
This ties to Easter in April as the "March saying" is practically emphasizing,
Lamb of God is Jesus Christ, and Easter celebrates his rising,

If the meanings of coloring, hiding, and finding eggs *during* Easter were analyzed,
Vivid coincidences would reveal what happened after Jesus Christ was crucified,
Eggs are pure with white; they're dressed up, hidden, and then joyfully recovered,
Decode that and you get a modern day definition of when Jesus Christ was rediscovered.

Holy Proof

If You Don't Have Someone

Expensive cars are like big rolling paper weights,
And mansions feel like giant empty wooden crates,
A dream is a lot of lost mental images, while an achievement is another, "ho-hum,"
As loneliness converts your heart into a dry prune, as it used to be a juicy plumb,

If you don't have someone...

The interior occupancy of any vehicle feels like it only has the driver's seat,
When your eyes look to the passenger side, & find no other eyes to meet,
Loads of money are just famous faces on fancy colored paper,
And as everyone else sees a sunny day, *you* see a storm that will never taper,

If you don't have someone...

A five star cruise that always exalts,
Would seem as stupid as a one person waltz,
A profession seems to be no different than daily chores,
And the sweetest chocolate is sour in a melted smores,

If you don't have someone...

You will always fail to see a beautiful bright sky,
That is until, a would-be sweetheart greets you with, "hi."
So this implies that life's many pleasures, & all of the world's gold,
Would be truly worthless, *if* you don't have someone... to hold.

<u>I'll Tell You</u>

I know it bothers you when we're on the street & people look at us a certain way,
And it is only when we're together, so, it makes you turn to me and say:
"What are they looking at? Why do they always stare?"
I'll tell you: "Let them see what we're capable of, 'cause in the long run? They won't care!"

It's the same thing when we're walking hand in hand, trying to enjoy our day,
You notice them whispering to each other as they occasionally glance our way,
You then look into my eyes as your face tells me that you're feeling guilty,
I then softly pass my hands across the skin of your cheeks, that feel so warm & silky,
That's when I'll tell you: "Don't worry about whatever it is they are saying over there,"
"Because by the time they leave our sights, they simply will not care!"

And baby, when I kiss you passionately in public, with a wanting swirling tongue,
Don't be so quick to stop me because there are no sexual alarms being sprung,
Don't tell me that this is something we really shouldn't do in front of public eyes,
Because when we were together innocently, our *every* move would hypnotize,

That's when I'll tell you: "It doesn't matter if what we do makes people whisper or stare,"
"We can show them that we have an over abundance of passionate energy to share,"
And then this is when I'll ease your worries after this next thing that I'll tell you,
That baby, "They simply don't care enough about each other to do the things that *we* do!"

Lottery

It lures people to it with its saying of, "All you need is a dollar and a dream,"
But its slogan of, "Hey, you never know," makes winning it as possible as it could seem,
There is nothing like the thought of potentially winning a multi-million dollar lottery,
That would allow anyone to shape their life as easily as soft clay molded into pottery,

I remember one of the many times that I gave in to its life changing illusion,
As my thoughts made me sink further into the "quick-picked millionaire" delusion,
If I'd win, I would no longer have lonely nights being serenaded solely by crickets,
So upon me thinking this, I went to a participating store and bought $2 worth of tickets,

Right after I left the store I began to feel the pains of being famished,
As my stomach craved meat being flame broiled, and then sandwiched,
But for me allowing my eyes to lead me into using $2 to be a fictional lottery winner,
I was short those same $2 that I could have used to buy myself a more decent dinner,

Thinking about what could be done after winning a lottery could make any sad face beam,
But I feel it's meant to take a bit of what could help to sustain you for your next dream,
People say, "You gotta be in it to win it," and that allowed me to "dream" of a new beginning,
But being that my finances are in a load of shit, *that* is exactly what I keep "winning."

So the lottery's slogan for my eyes now reads: "Hey! You? Never! NO!"

Match three like images, and win it.

LOTTERY 20046357

Love's Effect

After love's effect I saw my work ethic go from 40 to 400 percent,
As I was in the beginning of love's high altitude cruising ascent,
It is better than any type of proven aphrodisiac,
And I am no longer a pale romantic hemophiliac,

At this moment, my love clotted heart cannot detect any kind of hateful "ism,"
As any light turns into a passionate red as it passes through love's prism,
Finally, love's effect, something I thought I would *never* feel!
As I taste its fine wine, decorated caviar, & prestigious veal,

Love's effect, sent to earth by God as a heavenly relic,
Where every hug and kiss is *definitely* angelic!
When marriage isn't viewed as a hindering apparatus,
But a celebration of reaching love's highest rank & status,

Every problem of life no longer falls as hardened boulders of hail,
When you're serenaded into a dream by love's very own nightingale,
Love's effect, a feeling of entering heaven's own relaxing park,
Love's effect, a sensation that gives every heart a joyous mark.

Loving You

My dearest love, I am writing this to answer some of your deepest questions,
As I am sure you swore that I thought of them as "pestions,"
Well, I never have, but I was waiting for the right moment,
For when I could truthfully express myself with loving enjoyment,

There were times that I would do things that seemed so minute,
As your face practically read, "This male action just does not compute,"
You asked, "Why would you go out of your way to give me something so measly?"
Well, it was because I wanted you to *1*see that, loving you is easy,

My abysmal sense of amorous energy was the only thing I would consult,
As it showed me that the action encountered is not as important as the end result,
You asked, "How come you sometimes said things that sounded just plain cheesy?"
I just wanted to say them as they exited my heart, so you could *2*hear that, loving you is easy,

I wanted you to be exposed to love's ease, even through life's prosperity or hardships,
Loving is as simple as making toast sweetie, and not like navigating a fleet of starships,
I know you've asked yourself personally, "What did I do to make him act so breezy?"
Enough for me to strive towards making you *3*believe that, loving you is easy.

It's as easy as *1, 2, 3*.

<u>Men Like Me</u>

I'm at work getting *nothing* done, because I am thinking so damn much,
About how a lot of women really want an honest man that they could clutch,
My experienced older brother says that women are "starving" for men like me,
So many women! In countries from the letter A to Z,

Men like me are the kind that women thought to be extinct,
Men like me, who are so frightfully distinct,
Men like me, who actually totally give a damn,
Men like me, who see a female and *not* a leg of lamb,

And one thing that is happening nowadays which brings me a great concern,
Is men like me slowly changing after every crash and burn,
This then leaves those really sweet women thinking otherwise,
And feeling that every single man sees them only as a sexual prize,

So:
Men like me, aching to prove what they're worth,
Men like me, still present but, slowly dying off the face of the earth,
Men like me, forced to keep their hearts & emotions in shadows,
Men like me, practically being re-executed on love's guillotine after its gallows.

<u>My Beautiful Child</u>

On your date of birth I felt this, "rejoicing" of all my body's cells,
My abundant tears of joy could fill buckets, reservoirs & wells,
As I hear you drinking from your bottle while I look beyond our front porch,
My genes glow with an olympic pride, as they've *finally* passed along their torch,

It takes my breath away to see some of my traits starting anew in your traits,
As I fear that some of my weights will also be your weights,
But despite that, I'm so anxious to witness your first words & your first steps,
I'll be there for you from when the sun rises to long after it sets,

I would face any danger to keep you safe, because if there's one thing that's apparent,
Is that no beautiful child should *ever* be outlived by their parent,
I love you my beautiful child, and I'm not ashamed to say it aloud,
For you have made me incredibly happy in the years that went, and *so very* proud,

You've grown to become a mature and responsible adult,
No words can truly describe the emotional impact of that result,
I know the roads that led us to this point were up, down, & bumpy,
And believe me when I say that it pained me to see you upset or grumpy,

I forgive you for all the times you made me cry as if my eyes were sprayed with mace,
And upon you leaving the house angry & returning, made me relieved to see your face,
Now that you're moving on... well, I hope you don't mind me calling you each day,
Because I frequently get the same feeling I felt that first time I let you go out to play,

It's a feeling of emptiness that only your voice's acknowledgement can fill,
As now it'll be through a telephone more often, as opposed to a door or windowsill,
But my beautiful child, the biggest fulfillment of knowing that you've flourished & thrived,
Is the overjoying fact of me knowing that I'm survived,

Well, there is actually one more thing that could multiply that feeling times two...
And that would be for me to be able to witness who will be surviving you,
So before I stricken you with the inevitability of bereavement,
It would be beyond any words for me to hold your greatest achievement,

Just like your grandparents and I... held *you* as mine ... my beautiful child.

My Beautiful Child

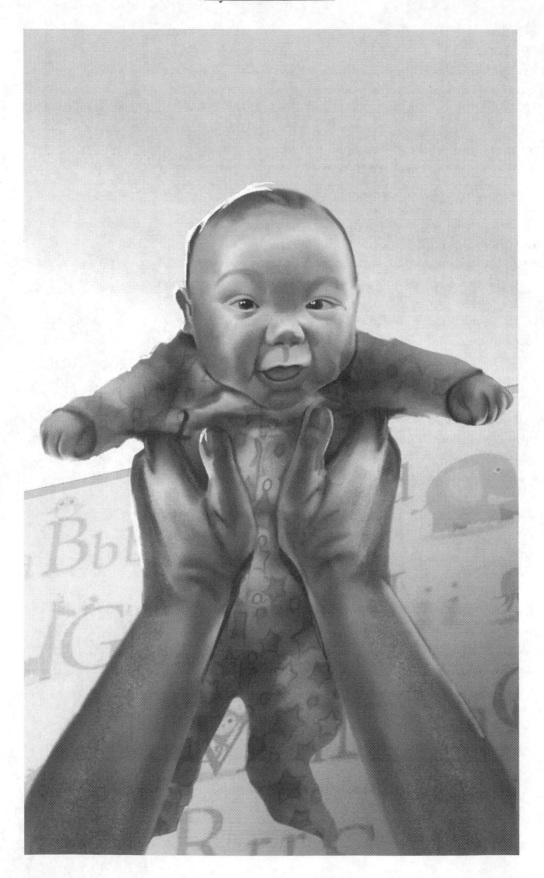

My Hispanic Women

All they have to say is, *"Hola mi amor,"* and I become like putty in their hands,
And I am *so* attracted by their hair as they love to color it in strands,
Yes, my Hispanic women are gorgeous and *very* elegant,
As that beauty instills fear into a man, a lot like a mouse to an elephant,

They are very well built, and they often feel like all men just want their "asses,"
They're so cautious towards men because their hearts are as fragile as glasses,
My Hispanic women feel like no single man knows this but, I do,
As most of them understand my approach much like a pigeon's coo,

I hate that because, all I want to do is pamper them with loving snuggles,
And I know that only my Hispanic women will understand our culture's many struggles,
They know the "language barrier" & what it is like to be categorized as, "a poor minority,"
As I often see how they place family values as their number one priority,

Such a shame to see them so young and rebelliously absent minded,
As all of the fun they are having now makes them walk around so blinded,
It appears that a lot of them love trying to make a man's sane mind go manic,
And most times my *Hispanic* women become just *that* ... "His-PANIC!"

But that is actually a small price to pay when considering their passionate spice,
As that curry like heat can quickly transition itself into shoulders of ice,
Because my Hispanic women treat me as if I was an invisible man at a corner standing still,
And if *they* can't see the good in me, then, I feel like no other culture of women will.

My Mind

I have you in my mind 24/7, as I am mentally converted into a porter,
Because I feel like if I'm toting luggage for Mr. Attention Deficit Disorder,
But it's not bad because, I drift away, in a beautiful daydream about you,
And upon it being broken I go, *"What?! Where?! When?! Who?!"*

In my mind, I have made love to you a number of times too numerous to count,
And respectfully supported your waist to place you on a horse you couldn't mount,
It's a place where I gently washed your feet in a calm & sparkling pond,
It is an area where I knew we would share the strongest bond,

There is definitely another realm, located deep within my mind,
No marriage licenses exist here, or prenups looking to be signed,
Here is where I gently wake you with the smell of breakfast in bed,
As the love story you once wished to be in no longer needs to be read,

Neurons are stars here, as they form a constellation of you in every lobe,
This is the only place I can be encircled by you like a warm inviting robe,
Mental images of you always center my heart when it gets misaligned,
But I only experience these things in a synapse, *deep* within my mind.

Nice Guys Finish Last

In my quest to find a special someone, there is one saying I have come across,
It is a saying used mostly by women, and as frequently as their lip gloss,
The saying is the sincere question of, "Why do nice guys finish last?"
I've seen it in on-line dating profiles, & even heard it shouted from atop a ship's mast,

Well, here are some of my points of view to this hypocritical question,
A woman would like an affectionate guy, but without fear of obsession,
A nice guy will let things slide more often than a clumsy penguin on ice,
This shows a woman that his authority would be obscured, and *not* precise,

Women are afraid that those, "nice guys" will smother them like a strangler,
As women are actually somewhat turned on by male aggression and anger,
A woman actually does not like being treated like some kind of celebrity,
It sparks boredom towards a man, as she would much rather be shown integrity,

Nice guys are also affiliated with: no spontaneity, no excitement or a dull thrill,
And this definitely goes against a young woman's "grab life by the horns" kind of will,
Women want a guy to be like water, in which he can be gentle enough for a bubble bath,
But sometimes strong enough to put her in her place with an overpowering tidal wrath,

A nice guy loves to show his reliability while ensuring that his promises are guaranteed,
A nice guy will always be little of what a woman wants, but all that she'll ever need,
Some women have this current "dog" notion on men, and they're just no longer trusting,
They feel that all men see love's heart as, "doggy style," because men just "can't stop lusting,"

Ladies, nice guys approach you the way they do because they want you to feel greeted,
What do *you* women do? Ignore them, shoot them down, or begin acting conceited!
There is *NO* man in this world who will notice your mind or heart first than your body,
Because your body is a window to your soul, *and,* every guy wants to be with a hottie, ☺

It won't matter if a nice guy greets you in English, Spanish, Italian, French or Finnish,
It shouldn't even be a question about being last anymore, as "nice guys" don't even finish!

When women wonder about the "nice guys," but then find themselves with the baddest boys on the block, they have no-one to blame but themselves! Need I say more about the "nice guy" question being hypocritical?

Notice Me

There are some days in which, I break down, and get so very sad,
That it turns me off towards listening to music or sporting a stylish fad,
I also turn myself off to the world, and my mind is gone indefinitely,
But deep down inside, I *really* want for someone to just... notice me,

As I am standing somewhere hurt, I ... I really want for someone to comfort me,
If I shout at someone to leave me alone, I ... I wish for them to say, "no" & stay with me,
When I'm frying with emotion as if I am touching an exposed electrical prong,
I really want someone to come beside me and softly ask, "Hey, what's wrong?"

Notice me...

Sometimes this particular sadness stems from the way in which I look,
As I feel ugly and unwanted, with value compared to that of bait on a fishing hook,
There are times that I wear everyday casual clothing or a nicely tailored suit,
And these are the times in which I really want someone to say that I look nice, or even cute,

Because sympathy or compliments from people really make you feel like they notice,
And soft words make an injured heart heal faster because they dress it with poultice,
It is then that I am placed on the road to recovering from my sad emotions,
As my body realizes that there would be no reason for teary eyed convulsions,

If a compliment is generous and uplifting with a highly pleasant style,
It can make a frown turn upside down, and then stretch it out for a mile,
When empathetic words reconnect my broken spirit as easily as a bunk bed's mortice,
It is *then* that—deep inside—I feel much better, because someone took the time to notice.

Took the time out of *their* own personal problems and their *own* personal life to notice ... *me.*

Politicians

I don't know what all these "tax hikes" are *really* about,
But, in doing that, politicians are practically saying: "Poor people get out!"
If politics were like a game of chess then, a politician would be a transparent pawn,
I say that because there are many times when no-one knows which side they're on,

When they run for office they practically brainwash people with, "I'm for you" schemes,
And after winning they secretly work at fulfilling the ideas of the rich & their dreams,
Politicians want people to focus on their lips when they say that there'll be no new taxes,
Probably so everyone doesn't notice the body parts crossing the origin of an x and y axis,

They get up on a stage to deliver their lines from behind a speaker amplified podium,
If people believe politicians then maybe they also believe canned foods have no sodium,
However, they're not all bad, and some should be commended for their bravery,
Starting with the ones who were against totalitarianism & the ones who abolished slavery,

But I have to say that, politicians these days have become way too hypocritical,
Their speeches tend to be on point, with views sounding *so* clear and analytical,
But that is a tactic the majority of them use to get their names high up in the polls,
And once they're in that office seat, they will treat votes & requests like toilet paper rolls.

Purification

There are times in our lives that bring about the greatest kind of frustration,
And we could never think of those times as being a means of purification,
I currently work a job that makes me feel like its sole purpose is to overwhelm,
As if it wants me to guide my life's ship to disaster, as it fights me for the helm,

There are so many times that I wanted to quit my job despite any ramification,
But this kind of job is meant to be stressful, as it is a means of purification,
Because now my mind is thinking of other things that I could do better,
It forces me to plan future goals as it'll ultimately convert me into a "go-getter,"

It brings me down *just* enough that I automatically agree with a chagrin nod,
I feel it does this to enforce the, "Eat from the sweat of your brow" curse from God,
And this type of purification doesn't just work with jobs,
It can also send people to help dispatch prides with high arched lobs,

For they will provide the beginnings of a much needed stimulation,
So that you could act off of the effects of your scheduled purification,
The same way an all-star football player is flogged with words after his careless fumble,
Purification is a similar thing that exposes each person to the feeling of, "humble,"

So from the average person, to a famous celebrity, to even the most successful CEO,
Will have some form of purification in life, that they & we all must undergo.

Receiving End

Some people have asked me, "Why do you do this?" and, "Why do you do that?"
"Why do you compliment some people who are just plain ugly and fat?"
I tell them that it is because I like to think that every person's heart is like a jewel,
And I like to live my life following and exercising the golden rule.

What about you? Have you ever been complimented at one time? How did it feel?

Same goes at my current job when I go above and beyond to please customers,
As I know that the smallest thing can offset them, like wind to floating gossamers,
A co-worker then ridicules me for making myself appear like a company mule or goat,
But a customer's treatment results to a company—and jobs—going under, or staying afloat.

What do you think? Were you ever treated as a valued customer? If so, what went through
your mind?

This deep appreciation I have for women will never diminish,
It is a fire that their icy rejections have yet to extinguish,
I'll never fathom their moments of discomfort from a hormonal tug of war,
This is why I'm *always* chivalrous towards women for being what they are & more!

So how about it ladies? Did anyone ever appreciate you? Where did it place your heart?

Unfortunately, there will *always* be this absurd rivalry between men,
No matter if the duel is with a sword, a gun or a pen,
But instead of having a feeling to hurt, maim or dissect,
I demonstrate a bigger showing of the utmost respect.

Think about it for a second guys. Has anyone ever totally respected you?

All of these things are occurrences that I've been exposed to quite a lot,
As I allowed myself to absorb them *all*, either later on, or on the spot,
My feelings, my mind and my heart all shared one notion they could not suspend,
That things become extremely different when it is *you* who is on the receiving end.

At the receiving end of someone's compliments, consideration, appreciation, respect, and other things that just makes your soul feel great.

Roses

Many people have often heard the term, "Stop and smell the roses,"
Upon that term being spoken some people strike "I don't get it" poses,
Much like life's moments, a rose is beautiful, even with the thorns close to its base,
And a rose is the most widely used flower because it gracefully adorns any space,

Life is so similar to a rose's attributes,
From the petals all the way to the roots,
The life span of a rose is short, no matter if it's in a vase of water or wine,
And a rose's color is powerful in representing a moment's message or sign,

So cherish your significant other as if it were the first week you got 'em,
And after you kiss that person take a step back and look at them from top to bottom,
Understand that the person looking back at you trusted in your affectionate words,
As that person accompanies you through streets of distant cities or suburbs,

Stop and smell the red rose of earned love.

If you're behind the controls of a road vehicle or an aerial craft,
Take a moment one day and look at it from fore to aft,
Understand that not too many people can operate a machine of that magnitude,
Think about this for a second during a safe velocity or altitude,

Stop and smell the gold rose of privileged skill.

Roses are often used for admiration, appreciation or emotional quelling,
Roses of life are things that require some time of a good & profound smelling,
Because life teaches us about its moments in ways that are horrifying, mysterious or clever,
In that everything considered to be great and fulfilling just doesn't last forever,

Hence the black rose of eternal farewell.

The hardest part is stopping to smell them without feeling rushed to get to a job or without being worried about problems in your life. The rushing & the worrying will always be there, but the "roses" won't.

She Says

I start with modest words, but I immediately get cut,
Even though my intentions are *far* away from smut,
I wish "yes" from their mouths was as abundant as candies from PEZ,
The following happens to me, and each exclamatory quote is what *she* says,

I try to greet one girl, and it goes: "Well hel—" *"NO!"*
I try to use the morning on the next one, but it becomes: "Good—" *"NO!"*
I try to compliment another girl after, but it's: "You look—" *"UH, NOT INTERESTED!"*
As I soon begin to feel like my forehead has an "L" that was skin crested,

And the funniest thing yet that was once randomly thrown at my face,
Is upon getting acquainted with a girl, she blows me off "just in case,"
So before *any* spark of interest she says, "We have nothing in common Raymond,"
If food could speak then, I'm sure that's what chocolate said to an almond,

Funny how chocolate with almonds is now one of the best mixes ever,
I really wish women would look closely before dropping their "no" lever,
But then again I wish for a lot of things, like love ironing my wrinkled life with a crease,
As what she says assures me that my rejections from women will never seem to cease.

Soldier Of Love

I thought that being good to a woman was something I should flaunt,
How I open all doors for her, from the car to the restaurant,
But then she'll look at me with a face filled with disdain,
So... damn baby, it seems you don't know so, I will explain,

I am a man in this world who is classified as, "Of a dying breed,"
The one that wants to be your fresh flower, and *not* a dirty weed,
For I am a soldier of love, trained by drill sergeant cherub,
To feed you strawberries in rich chocolate, not imitation carob,

So when I massage your back, kiss your cheeks, or rub your feet,
It is me trying to be neither gentle, kind, nor sweet,
It's just that, I am a soldier of love, prepared to pamper,
To make you feel comfortable & pleased, like a happy camper,

It doesn't matter if I was about to watch one of my favorite movies or concerts,
I'd leave right away if you asked me to go buy you kotex pads or tampon inserts,
Because I am a soldier of love, conditioned to provide,
To comfort your body, both on the surface *and* inside,

I'll take the deepest vow and stand with you in every fight,
I'll *never* be a man who'll treat you malicious or impolite,
I am the kind of man who will actually look forward to your maternity,
So you can be exposed to the loyalty I plan to give you for *all* eternity.

Because *I am*, your soldier of love!

STDs

Here is something I hope is being spoken about along with "the birds and the bees,"
About how if people are not conscientious, they can contract STDs,
You have to tell them to be careful how they share their sodas or slurpees,
Because you just don't know who could be walking around with dormant herpes,

Before you tattoo a lover's name on your body, and make it look like a large insignia,
You have to check yourself first to make sure that person didn't give you chlamydia,
Because you just never know if that person is a polygamous sexual hound,
And it would be unfortunate if you contracted it each time you both fooled around,

It is hard to resist the sensation of raw sexual stimulus,
Just hope you don't pay the price of pubic lice or syphilis,
Make sure that "keeping the lights on" is a part of your sexual idea,
So that you don't miss the clues of someone having genital warts or gonorrhea,

You have to steer clear of the dirtiest bird or the filthiest bee,
Before you get cursed with a slow killer in the form of AIDS or HIV,
They are diseases that basically just destroy the word "immune,"
And once you realize their symptoms, you *will* feel like a huge buffoon,

Because there was a chance to prevent it all with either abstinence or a condom,
Or, you could've taken your lovers to a free clinic before you decided to bond them,
Don't let your hormones or libido get the best of you, so be careful & mature,
Feel lucky if you contracted a treatable STD, but don't forget that others have *no* cure.

So think of protecting yourself before you open or erect yourself!

Straight Or Gay Way

This is an age of a new type of mentality,
A period now flourishing with homosexuality,
Mainly because hetero people gave the same sex a try,
And now consider themselves to be either fully gay or, "bi,"

The way I see it, in a reproductive sense:
If a woman gets penetrated by another woman then, she won't get a family in return,
And if a man is penetrated by another man then, all he'll get is an anal burn,
I respect them in various ways because, I, am not homophobic,
As I can pretty much hear, "*Me*, gay?! I have a better chance of becoming anaerobic!"

I don't get the whole "coming out the closet" thing but, I can understand, "being gay,"
And have uncovered articles claiming that it can be genetic in some way,
But what I have *really* noticed is that, many straight people walk around looking all bitter,
Being like cats with an urge to defecate, but still waiting around for that "perfect litter,"

Not finding that "perfect litter" can sometimes make someone go the opposite way,
And accept that loving comfort they are looking for from a person who is gay,
Or how about some insanely bright individuals that the "beautiful people" neglected?
As they were judged time & time again, while getting their foreheads stamped with, "rejected,"

Those people then walk sexually confused through love's alleyway,
And find the amorous attention they need from someone who is gay,
Hetero people should learn something from gays before throwing them for a loop,
For their rainbow means love, attention, and acceptance within all colors of their group,

Until we straight people adopt these ways in our group, without a cocky groan,
We will continue being bitter, while actually forcing *ourselves* to be alone,
So instead of looking at someone as a walking defect,
Know that there is no such thing as Ms. or Mr. Perfect.

Regardless if their way is straight or gay.

If a place of love is what you seek, then love will provide
the path to it that is best suited to the way your heart wants
to be.

Suicider

WAIT! Please just, hold on suicider!
Don't spill your blood like a broken jug of apple cider,
Throw away the death that is found in that killing pill,
Because you won't see your corpse, but if you do this then, I will,

And I don't want to see you on the news or in a daily printed article,
Lifeless, after your body was penetrated by a deadly particle,
That one thing that is bothering you will *always* overwhelm,
And imagine that same thing around you all the time in the other realm,

Suicide is a one way ticket to hell, as the devil laughs at those fatal stunts,
And the instant you're in his clutches then, you'll feel every kind of pain all at once,
So please, step down from the railing of that bridge,
Stop the car before it drives over that deep ridge,

Flush the syringe down the toilet along with those dirty drugs,
Feel the emotion as the people who love you cry out for your kisses & hugs,
For they know that a shattered jar of porcelain can be substituted with any other vase,
But a person with a living soul is a creation that *nothing* can replace!

<u>The Hints Of Her Want</u>

She doesn't want to show it but, there is something that she wants,
Her body is trying to spell it out, but her man sees unfamiliar fonts,
She looks to give him hints in the movies where those wants have starred,
Showing a fragile & soft female body feeling male muscles that are strong & hard,

How she bites the nail on her index finger at the sight of a long barge,
As now something narrow & small yearns for something wide & large,
But he sees this and ultimately ruins her fellatious mood,
Because instead of rushing her to a bed, he tells her, "let's get some food,"

So she is taken to a popular restaurant that is always candle lit,
And orders a piece of cake, then takes a fork and carves a slit,
The slit led to an empty spot that resembled the rounded shape of a cherry,
But he just thought it was a cute & playful way to joke with a berry,

The instant he patiently signaled the waiter to bring him the bill,
She looked shocked, due to the possibility of her not getting her night's fill,
So she just comes out and says it, because he missed each sign her body drew,
She grabs the back of his head and shouts, "YOU FOOL, I WANT TO SCREW!"

The Most Important Date

There are always frequent talks about many ancient prophecies,
That speak about coming periods of hardships & political hypocrisies,
Most of this talk led to the date of 12-21-2012 directly,
A date that the Mayan calendar chose selectively,

There was then a lot of talks about a civilization known as, "The Maya,"
Whose calendar instigated a "death date" of our precious mother Gaia,
In scripture it says, "the end of the world will come like a thief in the night,"
A saying like *that* is hard to swallow, let alone even bite!

But a thief surely doesn't work in a frozen state of poise,
A thief in the night *is* quiet, but ultimately makes a bit of noise,
So bits of the "noise" were talks about this inevitable planetary doom,
Along with books about surviving 2012 that continued to spread such gloom,

Then came talks of a "Nibiru," a "killer sunspot," or a "polar shift" holding true,
That will force us to care more for each other as there would remain so little few,
This would be necessary so that "truth" could be given to what some call a "biblical myth,"
About how humans were *not* created to be enemies with each other to begin with,

Then people spoke about how us uniting would make aliens see how our peace has evolved,
And that they'd make contact with us to show us how every single problem can be solved,
But then it was said that if these beings came with hidden agendas to enslave & deprive,
Then *all* humans would have to come together completely, in order to survive,

So if it would've taken this now false cataclysmic event to rid the earth of human hate,
Then, December 21st, 2012 would have forever been the *most* important date!

The date in which humans actually believe & show each other that they truly *are* one race.

Just once would I like to see some discovered ancient relic of prophecy show and tell of some *really* good news for a change.

Trophy Girls

There are regular women in the world, and then there are, "trophy girls,"
Females that seem as pointless as vanilla ice cream with vanilla icing swirls,
They are drop dead gorgeous, with bodies so incredibly shapely,
They possess the type of attraction that all men admire greatly,

When some men compare them to normal women, there is only one thing they get,
A fantasy of penile bliss, even though some of those guys might be happily taken or set,
But a trophy girl is just a great figure of beauty with a limited use,
And hidden just behind her is a rope, with one end tied up like a noose,

But before they hang a particular man they'll first lasso his accounts, stocks, or bonds,
So that they can optimize their trophy colors of gold, silver, and bronze,
You see how some competing athletes feel if they don't come in first at the end of a race?
When one of these girls is the waiting trophy, he *won't* mind 2nd or 3rd place,

They are pure lust, and their "love" starts slick, but ends up being gritty,
Like a trophy, they have a maintenance cost to keep them looking so pretty,
What good are the trophy girls who can make a married man have an affair?
What good are goddess like looks when compared to a decent woman's heavenly care?

You picture a trophy and what does it do? It just stands and decorates a corner,
And once its use has lost all its value, it will be given off to another holder,
A trophy girl might make a man look accomplished but he'll feel empty to the core,
He'll admit her good looks but later question, "What else *is* she exactly good for?"

Ultimate Man

If dating women was like winning games then, I never had a winning streak,
But through that pain I now see what a great number of women seek,
Enter what they need ... the ultimate man!
Doing something *every* day, instead of being a lazy can,

Always up and ready for anything spontaneous,
Never wasting effort on things that are extraneous,
But there was something that I noticed as it was targeting my chest,
That the path to becoming an ultimate man is now a useless quest,

Because women no longer believe in any form of chivalry,
As they're surrounded every day by vicious male deviltry,
But as women convince themselves that good men are close to none,
I strive at trying to become the *only* one,

The one who would:
Support his woman if she's the definition of "fatter" or "thinner,"
Wait for her with a nice warm home cooked dinner,
Be so good for her, like a muffin made with the richest bran,
Renew vows with her 30 years later to forever instill in her mind that *I am* her ultimate man.

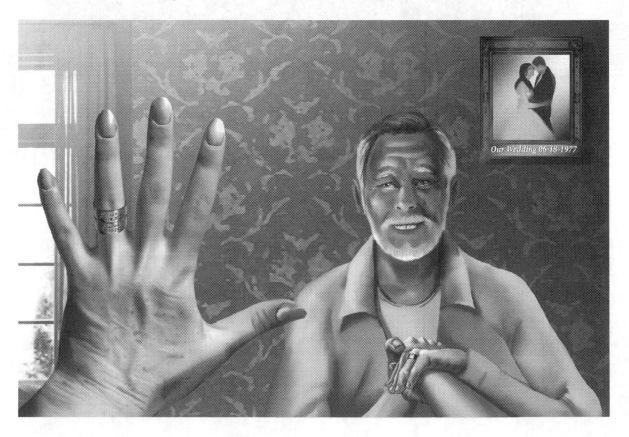

Under Superficial Beauty

They put on a show everytime they walk on the street,
Becoming just about every man's ultimate goal or feat,
A woman with the most *ridiculous* set of curves,
Will make a man higher than a ganja plant's herbs,

"Gotta have her" is all the man thinks as he is hypnotized with her butt,
As I ask him with my mind, "You want her *so badly* for what?"
Obviously only for the thrill of having the wildest kind of sex and nothing more,
The kind of sex that is not even practiced by the most untamed boar,

And so the men who fail to see under superficial beauty,
Get the biggest shock of their lives if and when they get the booty,
One hundred percent of beauty usually comes with a whole different view of smarts,
Or a vindictive woman that'll hang his ass on a wall & throw dildo shaped darts,

Hitting the rectal bullseye with every forceful throw,
And when she gets her way she'll shriek out like a dirty crow,
For every satisfied man that's with a woman that has intelligence higher up in her gene pool,
There is a man being traumatized by a beautiful woman, as she reveals her inner ghoul.

Unity

Some things were just *made* to be united,
Like candles with the fire that allows them to be lighted,
Like a vehicle with a skilled driver,
Or a pool with a graceful diver,

So many things go together to equal the perfect unity,
Like cultures coming together and forming a peaceful community,
Like peas mixing with carrots,
Like crackers and talkative parrots,

And then there comes females and males,
A unity more far reaching than boats and sails,
More conductive than outlets and electrical cords,
More complex than microchips & motherboards,

At this moment I just feel *so* alone!
And aching to listen to a soft female vocal tone,
I'm here fearing I will die without ever knowing when, or if she'll come
Especially with me knowing that the unity of "man + woman" equals the *perfect* sum.

War

Its pronunciation ruffles nerves if it comes from the mouth of a high ranking politician,
And then, soon enough, it sparks a destructive weapons exhibition,
Talks within a government body churns the butter of persuasion,
To take the next step and approve a large scale invasion,

Military forces are now like bulls being shown the color red,
As these bulls don't need to be provoked to charge, because they are led,
Winning the conflict is each opposing side's *greatest* wish,
Even if it means for one human to gut another human like a fish,

And so begins the most destruction & hate the world has ever known,
The sole actions that our all mighty God just cannot condone,

WAR!

<u>War</u>

So, *after* human lives were gambled with like a casino's roulette wheel,
Creatures of all kinds began to feast on their dead human meal,
Technology, resources, and submission are things "gained" once this conflict ends,
As the devil pins another notch on his belt that he so very cheerfully appends,

Crazy at how one country wanted to destroy another in an act of war,
Because now those once opposing countries have an open & friendly shore,
One now shows the other techniques for infrastructure & the values of a marketing guild,
As the stronger country, which leveled the other, now helps them to rebuild.

War?

We Latinas

We Latinas are known for being "fiery" and "spicy,"
If we don't like you then we'll show you the true meaning of, "icy,"
Treat us right and you'll get turned on more often than a light switch,
Cheat on us and you'll be introduced to a nightmarish, vicious, bitch!

We definitely justify the quote, "gets better with age, like a fine wine,"
We're often misunderstood, as *many* accuse us of being materialistically concubine,
But let's elaborate on the wine part so you can totally understand what we're about,
A little wine is good for your system, but abuse it & you'll be knocked the *hell* out!

We can look as soft as cotton, or as sharp as razors,
We come in *all* kinds of different shapes, colors and flavors,
There can be blonde hair, blue eyed Latinas, believe it, you can find us!
There are also dark skin Latinas with Asian type hair that look as exotic as a lotus,

We Latinas are born nurses as our care heals, from muscle sores to tooth decays,
Men desire us because they like voluptuous curves & not flat straightaways,
We like to show off the physical fruits of our ancestry, from African, Spanish to Taino,
Because we want our men to feel *damn* proud to be living as a Latino,

We love to cater for our special men and make them feel well-served,
We're enemies of noise when they're asleep, as we hate it when they're disturbed,
We Latinas are true lovers of the children in our families, regardless of *whatever* mixed race,
We love, care, cook & provide while living a life that moves at a fast pace.

We Latinas are destined to be in family roles that are as diverse as the culture that flows within our veins.

We Won, I Won

Here is another question to add to my usual daily queries,
About how some people get *so* excited from "their" baseball team winning the World Series,
"We won, we won!" Is what they say in every corner store or pub,
Wearing "their" team's logo as they go out to a movie or club,

So I had to ask a few of them, "What exactly did *you* win?"
"Is your favorite player gonna share with you their bonus cash or MVP pin?"
But they continue to celebrate as they point to what a newspaper's headline cites,
I look at them, shake my head & think, "All these crazed fans won were bragging rights,"

And living in New York, who needs a World Series championship, or any other championship
for that?

We Won, I Won

I have to be fair and look at myself to find something similar,
For I too have "self celebrated" with something in particular,
I love video games & practically play them until the controller becomes a part of my skin,
I look back at my own, "I won, I won" and now ask, "What exactly did *I* win?"

Because I truly did not win a battle/war, nor did I win the heart of a special fungi princess,
I didn't travel into space to deflect an asteroid that would offset the earth's precess,
What I *truly* did was save someone's game making job as they render a new game's sprites,
And as for me? Well, the only thing I truly won was my *own* type of bragging rights.

So ... *WE* WON!

I WON!

Whatever It Takes To Bring Us Together

It saddens me when a couple admits embarrassment at how they met,
Not thinking for one moment at how that occurrence was heaven set,
People, it doesn't matter if we get close in a call to consolidate a debt,
Or if we get acquainted from a website on the Internet,

Whatever bridges the gap,
And gets us on each other's map,
Just like the stitching needed to produce a jacket made of leather,
Whatever it takes to bring us together.

We need all the help we can get to cover the acres of love's land,
As we all know that love makes our lives go to exciting from bland,
So there is no shame in us meeting a person from being locked out of an apartment,
Or from our items hitting someone after they fell out of their storage compartment,

Whatever bridges the gap,
And gets us on each other's map,
Cupid knows of more ludicrous ways of binding two hearts in a loving tether,
Whatever it takes to bring us together.

There will be a joyous silliness in meeting through weird acts or stupid one liners,
As these will be the first things we remember once we reminisce as old timers,
It will be at that instant that our actions toward those moments will make us confess,
That we don't feel ridiculous about them now, but instead we feel loads of gratefulness,

Whatever bridges the gap,
And gets us on each other's map,
Just like the earth meets the sky from the sometimes crazy connection of weather,
Whatever it takes to bring us together.

The fiercest, most frightening thing can become oh *so* romantic when love is involved.

Write While I Cry

There are things that happen to me when I write while I cry,
I get into a mode where, the *smallest* detail won't pass me by,
Because I fall into a comatose type of meditation,
And the most minute thing receives my full consideration,

I imagine the process of a rich man becoming a humbled peasant,
As the same thing happens when my past becomes my present,
But beautiful energy comes to me when I write while I cry,
As the tears that fell on paper turn into words when they dry,

Never imagining that they could write something so profound & long,
Not to mention it taking the form of a sweet poem or gentle song,
My lacrimal glands never slow their secretions when I write while I cry,
As I actually enjoy my sadness when I ask God the question, "Why?"

Because deep down I feel so fortunate to even be alive to sense, "emotion,"
As the calming crispness of my tears go beyond being just a soul moisturizing lotion,
How I now have red scleras and sore retinas, aching to be in a state of REM,
But upon me looking at my paper, I realize that my tears have just polished a written gem.

There are things that happen to me when I write while I cry

Yielding Guilty Kiss

She was mine before, as I just kissed her for the first time in over three years,
A kiss so unpredictable that, it wouldn't have been visualized by seers,
Her mouth was so clean, warm and wet like just washed passion fruit,
It was a kiss *so* deep, one that only she could execute,

Her tongue covered mine like a soft love inviting quilt,
As my body was being filled with sexual arousal, along with guilt,
I got wrapped up in the moment of a mental reminiscing gush,
The feel of her brown sugar colored lips gave me *such* a rush!

The whole experience was as wicked as an evil witch's brew,
As one innocent kiss, soon enough, turned into two,
I would have stayed there kissing her for as long as I could,
This being the first time I did something so bad that felt *so* good,

The ambiance after her aphrodisiacal kiss was a feeling of floating in tepid air,
But then a deep fear struck me as if I was a naked knight in a dragon's lair,
For I was like a mouse braving a sleeping cat for a piece of satisfying Swiss,
The moment I accepted the offer of a married woman's yielding guilty kiss.

<u>Your Creative Work</u>

Creator, the world is your audience, half will *always* be pro and the rest will be con,
It is instinctual for you to show them what turned your creative bulb on,
Being successful from doing creative work you truly love is totally fulfilling,
And it is okay to hope to earn lots of money from it as, we *all* need to make a living,

Just put it out there, no matter if it's with a shove, a push, or a nudge,
Put your creative work out there, and let the whole world be the judge,
Don't get discouraged by 1, 2, even 1,000,000 haters or critics,
With their icy reviews and hurtful bad mouthing gimmicks,

The world is inhabited by *billions* of people, and they are largely diverse,
What will be a blessing to one, the other will see it as a curse,
There will always be 50% of people who will love you, no matter what,
Then there will always be the remaining 50% who'll hate you down to your gut,

Be your *total* self, so that the ones who *will* love you see that you possess a lot of clout,
Be your total self so that the ones who will hate you start getting weeded out,
So if you create movies, books, music, or pastries covered with fudge,
Put your creative work out there, and let the *whole* world be the judge!

Because, "if you build it, they will come." But, you have to let them know it's there.

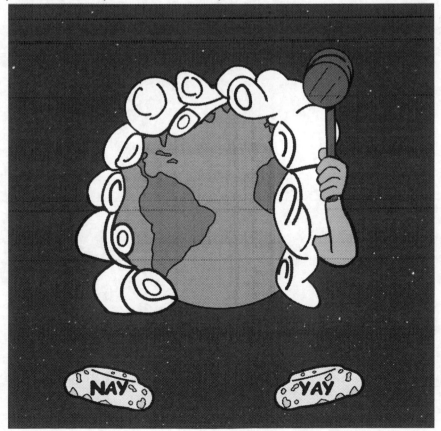

You're Invited

There comes a special moment in the life of every individual,
Moments that I would put under a category of "residual,"
Because some moments remain to be encountered, but as life goes on, they *are* reached,
And other moments just come without warning, as if a life's hull has been breached,

There are moments of graduation & celebration that are carefully ignited,
The kind of moments that beg to be shared by people as it begins with, "You're Invited,"
This is a time that I become sad for myself as I am happy for those who rejoice,
As a weird feeling comes over me accompanied by a mental voice,

"Look at them cheering and celebrating, but where is my position in all of this?"
"I am happy for them all but, *when* will it be *my* time to enjoy such bliss?"
"Every time I completed something grand, no-one celebrated things for me,"
"I never saw anyone taking home videos of my accomplishments to display later on TV,"

But then there is a moment that needs to come in a person's life at a *very* particular time,
Where they proudly know that the words, "the host of this" is started by the word, "I'm,"
When true love is found, a baby ultimately follows the quest of the combining two,
And when both people know that they are in love their souls shout a big, "Woo Hoo!"

Marriages and babies are things that I have seen everyone I grew up with undergo,
As a part of me feels *so* late to ever expect my very own "I do" & little one show,
A part of me wants to have a moment that will get family & friends very excited,
As I want that moment to beg to be displayed on a card, titled with, "You're Invited."

I feel that one of the *many* reasons why family & friends exist in human life is because, every now and then, we truly enjoy a good congratulated pat on the back.

Raymond A. Hiraldo's Quotes

"The best type of revenge is your continued success."

"A peanut paying job will keep bill collecting elephants at bay for the time being."

"Nowadays, when a man offers a woman the world, she'll set her eyes on the universe."

"The most counterproductive thing any active person can do is 'sleep.'"

"If you're helping people out of a financial hole, it is better to pull them out from the outside rather than be inside with them while they step on your head to get out."

"Sometimes you have to shock yourself into making a change in your life."

"When the heart is happy, the mind & everything else usually follows, even if it's foolishly."

"There will be moments in life when you need to be an asshole. Why? Because an asshole has an easier time dealing with shit."

"Sometimes life will have harsh ways of pointing you in the right direction."

"Volcanoes of creativity are similar to actual volcanoes in the fact that they all need 'pressure' to erupt."

"Not all poetry can be liked, but all poetry should be respected."

<u>Acknowledgements</u>

There is just absolutely *no* way I could have *ever* completed this book all on my own. Any, and I truly mean *any* individual would be lost if it weren't for the help, understanding, love and guidance of others. First & foremost, I want to thank God for putting me where I need to be. Even though I have yet to understand why I am where I am in my life, I'm sure he'll reveal everything to me at the proper time.

In no particular order, here are my other "thank you" recipients.

Trafford Publishing - For all the care they display towards the production of this second book. They have been great to work with.

My Mother & Father - They have dedicated their *whole* lives to the assurance of my well-being.

Domingo Canela Jr. - My best friend of over 15 years. The only time he has ever looked down at me was to pick me up after I fell.

Ivan Pushkov Vasilyevich - A talented, trustworthy and dedicated artist who stuck by me through this long project until the very end. He made all my wild and crazy art ideas become a reality.

Ivan can be contacted at: virtualjunk.tumblr.com & cyberduster@gmail.com.

And to all my readers/supporters, once again:

Thank You!